GW01231012

CONTENTS

Title Page	4
Copyright	5
Dedication	6
Introduction & Preamble	8
Chapter 1: Do you want to work in Politics?	10
Chapter 2: What sort of career options are there in politics?	17
Chapter 3: Preparing for Success	33
Chapter 4: Excellent CV Writing.	40
Chapter 5: Productive Job Hunting	48
Chapter 6: Finding Political Job adverts	55
Chapter 7: Interviews	61
Chapter 8: Other career options	75
Chapter 9: Final Thoughts	82
Selected Reading List	84

POLITICAL CAREERS

The secret & confidential guide to finding, applying and getting a job in British politics

By Joseph Henry

Political Careers by Joseph Henry

ISBN: 9798602355918

Copyright Joseph Henry

Published by HH Books - an independant inprint

Cover copyright of Joseph Henry

The Authors opinion is expressed thoughtout this book.

All rights reserved.

Although the author and publisher have made every effort to ensure that the information in this book was correct at press time, the author and publisher do not assume and hereby disclaim any liability to any party for any loss, damage, or disruption caused by errors or omissions, whether such errors or omissions result from negligence, accident, or any other cause. Please undertake your own detailed research and due dilligence.

This book is dedicated to Cathrine.

INTRODUCTION & PREAMBLE

Hello and welcome to my book, Political Careers, and the not-so-secret guide to finding, applying for, and getting a job in politics.

My name is Joseph Henry, and for over eight years I have been recruiting in the political sector, firstly for Electus Group, which was part of Dods Plc, and then my own outfit, Westminster Search (now Hopkins Henry).

Before this, I worked in both non-political recruitment and in politics. I had the joy of working within the Members of Parliament and the Members of the Scottish Parliament.

Working in politics was a fantastic experience that I would not trade for the world. It was a tough, challenging and very interesting experience.

After taking a mini-sabbatical to move house and enjoy some beautiful Scottish countryside, I decided to write a book to help people get into politics. I was inspired to help people who come from ordinary backgrounds to get a job in British politics. I hope to achieve this by making the key information available in one slim-line book.

The recent political crisis that formed around Brexit, coupled with my own experiences, made me realise that British politics needs more ordinary people from ordinary backgrounds at all levels. Although, this is no rallying cry for class war or bashing of the current political class.

It is based on an observation that, if at every level of British politics we had more people from ordinary backgrounds, our political and governmental system would be better placed to listen to and serve its people.

Our current MP's do a wonderful job, and most (if not all) work hard for their constituents. However, for a renewal of British politics to happen we need British politics to truly reflect those whom it seeks to serve.

My aim and hope for this book is to democratise & popularise the information around careers in politics in one easy volume so it is accessible for all. So people can see that there is more to a career around politics than getting elected, and can be a fulfilling career.

Hopefully, this book will play a small part in the great democratic story that the British Isles represents and inspire the next generation of researchers, caseworkers and advisers.

CHAPTER 1: DO YOU WANT TO WORK IN POLITICS?

"No matter where you stand politically - even if you're unsure of what your political ideology is - it is important to take part in the process of shaping our government."

Brad Henry - Former Democratic Governor of Oklahoma

Curiosity killed the cat, but knowledge brought it back. You are curious about getting a job in politics. Otherwise, I am unsure why you are reading this book. Buying this book has been an excellent investment as it will give you the knowledge to:

Help you get a job in politics.

Or put you off working in politics forever.

Either way, you either find the job of your dreams or save yourself wasted hours, days, weeks and possibly months pursuing a career path that was not for you, so it is Win-Win whatever happens.

So do you want to work in politics?

Do you really, really, want to work in politics, or have you fallen in love with the idea of working in politics?

These are two very different things.

In this chapter, we are going to highlight the things that make working in politics awful. This will be a "Debbie Downer" chapter. A whinge-a-thon if you will.

However, you need to be honest with yourself. Being honest with yourself will be the best investment you can make at this point. It will lead to you taking the better path instead of the wrong path and save yourself from wasting time. That's time that could have been spent playing Pokemon Go.

So now that I have your attention (unless you are playing Pokemon Go) let us begin.

Politics is hard work.

Politics is hard work as a job. It's a tough job. Not as tough as a coal miner in Siberia during November, I grant you, but it is very much a tough and demanding sector to work in.

Hard work is the nature of the beast.

Politics can be a hard job to work for a whole host of reasons: From the long and weird hours, the way that it invades personal life and how it destroys your love of politics. It can also be hard, as it feels like there is no escape from the daily madness that is

politics.
Politics is not popular.

People will not like your career choice - politics is not accessible or popular at the moment.

Politicians are not popular presently, and their staff sometimes get it in the ear quite a lot for working with them. Politics has always been an unpopular profession in the UK. There is something about the way that as a country, we have always disliked our politicians.

This atmosphere can become a grind, and politics will never be able to please everyone.
Lack of free time.

Working in politics, you will not have that much free time. It is all-encompassing career. It will take up other large amounts of your time, especially if you're working for an MP in Westminster. What we are talking about is a lot of evening and weekend work, and on occasion, you will be burning candles at both ends.

If you work in politics, expect to be time-poor.

Working 'in politics' ruins politics.

Before working in politics, I used to be a bit of a political nerd and loved watching politics like other people watch football. I am also an Arsenal fan, so clearly I am a glutton for punishment.

Question Time, PMQs, Sunday Politics, - I loved the lot and would watch loads of it. Politics seemed like the perfect career destination for me as premiership footballer was off the table. Once I got involved, it took away the veneer. It changed its appeal.

I presume this phenomenon is like people who love wrestling.

Then visit the wrestling training camp and find out just how fake it is. Sorry, not fake, scripted, totally scripted. That, of course, is a debate for another day, and another book.

Or as they say in Tennessee "wrestling isn't fake, people are".

Politics can feel inescapable.

Politics can be very stressful because you can't get away from it, there is no escape.

You can't read the paper without seeing it.

You can't read a magazine without mentioning it.

You can't turn on the radio without hearing about it.

You can't watch the television without the news popping up.

You certainly can not go on Facebook without seeing stuff about politics.

Even when you pop down the local corner shop for 20 Benson and Hedges and a pack of Frazzles, it is there in the headlines of papers as you walk in.

So switching off can be hard, which is stressful.
The pay is okay, not lucrative.

The pay is not massive in politics. It has gotten better of late. However, if you are money-motivated, then Politics is not really for you.

In a lot of other professions, you will be able to earn more, with less stress, ambiguity, less work and more fun.

If you are highly financially motivated, politics will not be for you.

MP's can be the best or worst line managers.

Now one of the fantastic things about working in politics is that an MP will be your boss and this is quite exciting.

However, they can either be the best employers you ever have, or the worst people you have ever come across.

This cuts across party lines. I have heard stories about numerous "bad bosses" in my time that work in politics from all shades and parts of the political spectrum. Some of them are rather surprising.

I was fortunate and had good bosses while working in politics. However, in general, the standard rules do not seem to apply in parliament like they do in typical workplaces. I think one of the best analogies is to think of an MP's office as a small family business. Some family businesses have the best working conditions others are just awful places to work.

The Civil Service has more influence than you realise.

This is not something that the press make much hay about. If you want real influence on how policy is implemented and actioned, the Civil Service or Local Government might be better destinations for you.

The world is too complicated, and organisations are too big even for ministers to have detailed insight into the day-to-day running of policy programs. So working for an MP can lead to work that is shallower than expected. Especially backbenchers.

Also, the work can feel at times it is more about cleaning up after the mess that the civil service or local town hall has created, as any seasoned caseworker can attest.

Politics - more 'The Office' than 'The West Wing'.

Politics always look so exciting on television. speeches, press junkets, walkabouts, debates, spin rooms and election night coverage.

Be in the 'West Wing or the 'Thick of It' there is an air of excitement and getting things done and changing the world. It is a world full of non-stop excitement and intellectual engagement, and no day ever looks boring, dull or unimportant.

However, this is just not real life. Politics is, sadly, just like any other job. It will, after a while, get boring and rather dull. If you want to watch a program that is a great model for politics, watch The Office.

Even the world's most exciting and thrilling job shall, in the end, become humdrum and run-of-the-mill. Politics is not immune to this phenomenon.

My theory is that politics is 95% The Office, 4% The Thick of It and 1% the West Wing.

So do you want to work in politics?

Has anything that I have written above put you off?

The time I spent working in politics was an interesting and exciting time. It was also the worst time I ever had - as well.

If you are willing to accept the above, working in politics brings a whole host of rewards.

Just do not expect it is how the TV or your imagination thinks it to be.

Now that I have been a misery guts, let's get onto the show and start talking about how you can get a role in politics.

CHAPTER 2: WHAT SORT OF CAREER OPTIONS ARE THERE IN POLITICS?

So you have decided that you still want to work in politics. Good, you survived the first test.

We did not want to be big 'Debbie' or 'Dave Downers'. However, we felt it was only right to give you an unvarnished look at working in politics.

There are lots of options to work in politics, the focus of this chapter will be on jobs in politics. Primarily focused on Political Parties, Local Councils, Members of Parliament, Members of the Scottish Parliament and Members of the Welsh Assembly.

However, this book is not about becoming a politician. It is not about becoming an MP, a Councillor, an AM or MSP or indeed a Police and Crime Commissioner. It is about working for an elected official only, not becoming an elected official.

If you are looking for that book, I would visit Amazon or your local bookstore - preferably your local bookstore.

The political ecosystem has gotten more prominent over the years, and after working for an MP, there is a new diverse range of roles available. However, we shall cover some of these in a later chapter of this book.

One of the exciting things about politics is that there is a wide diversity of job titles and responsibilities. This means that although job titles can be similar, on many occasions the responsibilities can be very different. The main overarching roles are as follows.

Caseworkers.
Researchers.
Campaigners.
Office Managers/Chief of Staff.

These are the principal career options when working for an MP.

From office to office, the responsibilities and structures of how the daily operations will be run are different. However, we are going to talk about these roles on a general level for ease of understanding.

Caseworkers.

Caseworkers are the forgotten heroes of British politics. They are the people who are closest to constituents and many live and work in the constituency that they serve.

Caseworks end up over their career dealing with a wide range of issues that are really at the coal-face of British politics: from dealing with complaints about planning application through to immigration issues and often via the occasional weird and wacky as well.

Since the birth of the internet age, there has been a real increase in organisations using digital platforms to lobby via constituents for issues of all stripes. This has lead to a heavy workload. However, also, this has become an essential process of bringing MPs and constituents closer together and highlight key concerns.

Much of the responsibility for dealing with the casework, whether it is writing letters to local council leaders to calling up a government department to chase up information, falls into the purview of the caseworker.

Much of the work which caseworkers do will require a large degree of pro-activity and self drive.

Many caseworks have helped save people from deportation, highlight miscarriages of justice through to helping numerous local people with local but important problems that can change lives.

For those who want to make a real impact day-to-day on local constituents' lives, this is the job for you.

Where to find these roles?

W4MP is the best website for looking for caseworker roles. Looking at Political Party career sections is also useful.

Payscales.

London

Caseworkers   £21,960 - £32,548,
Senior Caseworkers   £27,324 - £38,421

Outside London

Caseworkers   £19,641 - £28,804
Senior Caseworkers   £23,938 - £36,645

Example Job Advert.

Caseworker
London

The role will focus on constituency casework and policy correspondence and will involve dealing directly with constituents on a wide range of issues. It will include:

Corresponding with constituents about casework issues on behalf of the Member.

Providing information, advice and support to voters over the phone or in writing.

Liaising with central and local government organisations.

Maintaining accurate records.

Some policy casework with scope for development.

General office administration and support.

The following skills are essential:

A polite and professional manner.

Excellent communication and administrative skills.

The ability to make written representations of a high standard, accurately and concisely.

Competent use of IT (experience using casework processing software is desirable but not essential).

Literate with the Microsoft Office Suite, including MS Outlook and MS Word.

The ability to prioritise and manage a caseload efficiently.

Record keeping and dealing with confidential and sensitive information appropriately.

The ability to work independently, while also contributing to a small, tight-knit team.

Knowledge and understanding of the political landscape.

Upon appointment, you will be required to comply with the Baseline Personnel Security Standard, undertaken by the Members' Staff Verification Office (MSVO). See Members' Staff Verification Office (MSVO) page for further info. MPs generally pay staff following IPSA guidelines.

Parliamentary Researcher/Assistant.

If the caseworker is the workhorse of an MP's office in the local constituency, then the Parliamentary Researcher are the Labradors of British Politics. Everyone's got one!

The Parliamentary Researcher has to play researcher/speechwriter/policy adviser/political genius/sounding board/magician/general helper. It is a role which, during the high drama of British politics, can be a real tough ask, but also very exciting.

The Researcher will put together a wide range of briefings on policy and political developments, policy notes, press releases, press notes, parliamentary questions and other relevant materials, deal with the media both verbally and on top of all this become a generalist expert in numerous policy areas.

As a researcher, you will be required to keep up-to-date on Parliamentary Bills, Early Day Motions, political developments and upcoming debates on relevant issues. The Researcher is in many ways, the intellectual and operational force driving an MP's Westminster office.

You will also field a large number of calls from Lobbyists of all stripes. Trying to arrange meetings or promote new reports, ideas or events. So you'll also be a gatekeeper helping to prioritise your MP's busy schedule.

Occasionally, you might even have to carry a bag and grab a coffee (if the intern is on holiday!).

Where to find these roles.

Again W4MP is the best place to search for these roles, as is of course your political party website. As ever, please see later chapter for more information.

Payscales.

London

Parliamentary Researcher	£23,750 - £34,786
Senior Parliamentary Researcher	£33,000 - £49,793

Outside London

Parliamentary Researcher	£20,420 - £31,875
Senior Parliamentary Researcher	£30,290 - £43,881

Mr Joseph Henry

Example advert.

Parliamentary Researcher
Westminster

A vacancy for a Parliamentary Researcher, in this MP's office in Westminster. has arisen. The position would be perfect for a recent graduate with strong knowledge and interest in politics.

Responsibilities will include:

Supporting the M.P. in his capacity as a member of the prestigious Select Committee.

Preparing and presenting briefing notes for committees, press releases, parliamentary questions and other materials.

Undertaking research, usually from readily available sources, on straightforward and un-straightforward topics.

Being aware and updated on developments in the media relevant to your areas of responsibility.

Drafting written and oral Parliamentary Questions every week.

Developing and maintaining current knowledge of bills, debates, legislation, Early Day Motions, Hansard, etc.

Government policy casework, as depending upon requirements.

General administrative duties where required.

The successful candidate must have:

Clear interest in politics.

A high standard of verbal and written communication skills.

The ability to work to tight deadlines and complete tasks at short notice in a high-pressure environment.

Comfortable with working independently as well as part of a small team.

Loyalty and discretion at all times, on matters sensitive or otherwise.

Excellent IT skills, knowledge of Microsoft Office package, and the ability to adapt to new software.

Upon appointment, you will be required to comply with the Baseline Personnel Security Standard, undertaken by the Members' Staff Verification Office (MSVO). See Members' Staff Verification Office (MSVO) page for further info. MPs generally pay staff under IPSA guidelines.

Political Campaigner/Constituency Organiser/Community Campaigner.

When working in politics I was a campaigner, and I loved it. Working on local campaigns at the local level was great fun, if challenging. A Political Campaigner is generally a more overtly "party political" role than a researcher and caseworker. In many cases, the budget for such a function is funded locally by the local party or interested donors.

So what will you be doing as a Political Campaigner?

Mostly you will engage in a constant battle for awareness and attention of the local press and local constituents through a variety of campaigning mediums, actions and tactics. In short, you are keeping your MP and party front and centre in people's minds so they don't go "who?" when your boss is mentioned on the doorstep.

On a day-to-day basis, the workload can vary depending on the time of year and the point within the election cycle. However, a Political Campaigner will cover the following:

Creation of campaign materials.
Mobilisations and recruitment of volunteers.
Organising of action days.
Crafting of political messages.
Office administration
Fundraising for donations
And on election day, leading the 'Get The Vote Out' operations locally.

Where to find these roles?

Again W4MP is the best place to search for these roles, as are of course political party websites. As ever, please see later chapter for more information.

Payscales.

Given the nature and variety of these roles, salaries can range from £18,000 - £35,000

Example job advert.

Campaign Manager
Local Party Offices - Local Town

Key Responsibilities will include:

Leading production of creative and effective digital and printed communication to deliver our agreed literature plan.

Coordinating the work of local volunteers - ensuring we have an active and energised team of members and supporters strong enough to achieve our electoral objectives.

Leading and generating voter contact activity.

Collaborating effectively with the local party – and other partners supporting the local party's campaigns, and National Campaigns Department and other nearby local parties.

Supporting the management of the local party's electoral and membership data

Monitoring and responding to contacts via the office and the website.

We're looking for someone:

Who is goal-oriented: Setting and achieving ambitious goals.

Who is collaborative: Able to maintain productive relationships with key political stakeholders.

Who is motivating: Strong ability to achieve results via other people. Someone who motivates and energises volunteers.

Who is organised: Able to handle a large and varied workload. Someone who can set clear, practical priorities for themselves and others.

Who takes the initiative: Creatively identifies opportunities to deliver objectives.

Who shares our values: Sympathise with aims and objectives of the political party..

Essential skills

Campaigning: Practical experience of delivering political change and winning elections via active campaigning.

Desktop & Digital Publishing and Design: Production of robust literature via desktop publishing.

Computers: Confidence with word-processing and spreadsheets. Knowledge of databases preferred.

Experience of working with and motivating volunteers.

Financial management: Basic budget management.

Having a full driving licence and access to a car is desirable.

Office Manager.

Office Managers are the administrative and leadership heart of an MP's operation. Not all MP's have office managers, sometimes the senior responsibility ends up in the hands of a senior caseworker or a parliamentary researcher.

Generally speaking, Office Managers (if an MP has them amongst their staff) are likely to be based in the constituency rather than Westminster. This role will typically take on a wide range of responsibilities.

Where to find these roles?

W4MP and the career section of party websites.

Payscales.

Office Manager - London
£30,324 - £44,485

Office Manager - Outside of London
£27,815 - £40,633

Example Job Advert.

The successful applicant will work as part of a small team located in the constituency office, supporting their MP.

The candidate must be a highly organised individual. They must be a team player, have attention to detail, and HR knowledge/experience. Strong administrative, IT, interpersonal and communication (written and verbal) skills are essential.

Main duties include:

Comprehensive and efficient administrative and organisational support. This includes diary and events management, along with booking meetings/travel.

Processing expenses and registering financial interests promptly.

You are keeping accurate and orderly files.

Assisting with drafting, letters, mail outs and reports etc.

Providing support to the Senior Constituency Caseworker when required.

Writing agendas and itineraries for the Member, and ensuring he receives all relevant information before meetings/events in the constituency.

Ensuring accurate office and personnel records are kept up to date, and that information is managed confidentially and in line with GDPR.

HR, including recruitment tasks.

Updating the website with the member's constituency activities.

Ensuring adequate office supplies, working with suppliers.

Seeing through local campaigns ensuring stakeholders are informed to raise awareness of ongoing issues across the constituency.

Candidates should have the following skills and qualities:

Excellent communication, organisational and administrative skills, as well as experience of working in a small dedicated team.

Literate with Microsoft Office and including MS Outlook, MS Word, MS Excel and OneDrive.

Ability to use their initiative and manage/prioritise their workload.

Excellent team ethic with superb interpersonal skills.
Ability to work to tight deadlines.

Upon appointment, you will be required to comply with the Baseline Personnel Security Standard, undertaken by the Members' Staff Verification Office (MSVO). See Members' Staff Verification Office (MSVO) page for further info. MPs generally pay staff under IPSA guidelines.

Notes on Chief of Staff and other job titles.

Sometimes you will come across people and roles that are called

Chief of Staff or other grandiose titles that have existed. Generally, these roles are either combinations of office manager and senior parliamentary researcher roles.

Although it is a great sounding title, given the budget and staff size of the average MP, Chief of Staff is more of a title than a genuinely distinct role. Generally this title is more suited to large organisations with very large budgets and employees.

Note on Special Advisers.

Please note we have not included detailed information about becoming a Special Adviser to the Minister in the UK Government. The reason for this is simple, these roles are very rare (relative to the number of people working for an MP) and application processes for these roles change with each new government. Some of these jobs simply go to those working with an MP when they are promoted to ministerial positions.

Jobs with Local Councils.

Recently there has been a trend in Local Authorities & Councils to recruit support officers for political groups and the council leader. These are exciting positions that are great for people who might not want to relocate to the big smoke of London but still love politics.

What you will do in these roles varies significantly from day-to-day and council-to-council depending upon the structure and council size.

Where will you find these roles?

W4MP, Jobs Go Public, individual council websites and Guardian jobs.

Mr Joseph Henry

Payscales.

Various examples range £22,000 - £40,000 depending on role, council, and location.

Example advert.

Group Support Officer
Local Council

XXXXXXX Council is a Unitary Authority, governed by a leader and cabinet system. The XXXXXXX made gains at the recent elections and are the largest opposition party on the council. The XXXXX Party are the majority group.

We are looking for a highly motivated individual with exceptional political and communication skills working directly with the XXXXXX Group on the Council. Your role will primarily involve advising on political issues, and will also include dealing with the media, preparing speeches and briefing notes, researching policy issues, attending meetings and conferences within the area and elsewhere.

You will act as the focus for information gathering and dissemination with community groups, MPs, local authorities, commercial groups, and deal with Officers at all levels. Strong networking skills are essential to enable you to play a central part in the adequate preparation and delivery of the Group's future political strategy.

As a member of the XXXXXXX Party, you will bring acute political judgement, the ability to analyse data quickly, have excellent written and oral skills and good IT knowledge with real ambition to move the Party to its fullest economic potential.

The post is subject to political restrictions following the Local

Government and Housing Act 1989. Hours of work will include evenings and possibly weekends.

Jobs with Political Parties.

Political Parties are slightly odd organisations at an administrative level. In some respects, they are most akin to charities and other third sector organisations, with accounts, marketing, legal, policy, human resources, media relations, communications, campaigns, fundraising, digital, IT and membership departments.

This structure means that political parties are great career destinations for people who have already got career experience behind them and want to try politics.

Where to find these roles.

The best place to look for roles with political parties is on their own website.Please see the appendix section for further information.

Payscales.

Varies - the pay for roles in Political Parties can differ depending on the position, the level and the party itself.

For a better idea on salaries, please visit individual party political websites.

Example adverts.

Given the sheer diversity of roles in political parties, an example would be unhelpful. However, I would suggest you visit the appendix for political party websites to get a better appreciation.

CHAPTER 3: PREPARING FOR SUCCESS

So you have decided that you want to get into politics, you have an idea of the type of role you want. Now you need to prepare for getting a job successfully.

As the saying goes, Proper Preparation Prevents Poor Performance. Or as Tony Blair might have said it, "Preparation, Preparation, Preparation".

If you are going into politics as a career, then there are some steps that you need to take to help prepare for this journey.

The type of preparation depends upon your career stage. Mostly there are three career stages: Undergraduate, Postgraduate and Career Transition, for our purposes in this book.

We will discuss each of these areas separately. However, first we are going to address some of the usual preparations.

General Preparations.

Whether you are a newly minted graduate or are looking to make a career transition in your mid-forties, some universal rules will help your preparation for your new career:

Remember you need a good CV to help get your foot in the door (see our CV chapter).

Making connections can be useful - focus on these through activism and attendance at events and not just twitter.

Have a backup plan if a career working in politics fails to pan out.

Attend as many interviews as you can - so you are 'match fit' at the next interview that really matters.

Keep up-to-date with politics daily. Read up on politics daily beyond the headlines - use websites like Politics Home.

Volunteer with your local political party - being active locally and volunteering is important as British politics is 90% based on the action of volunteers.

Undergraduate Preparations.

So you are a bright-eyed and bushy-tailed undergraduate who is excited about getting a job in politics. Brilliant stuff!

You have more free time and energy than you know what to do with, and you need to start laying down the foundation for getting a career in politics. You might not realise it, but over the next three years you have the time to achieve a lot with more free time than you can imagine. Do not waste this opportunity.

Now, there is more to politics than joining your university's party association and engaging in vigorous debates over a pint of cider and black (I am so showing my age?). University offers a whole host of opportunities to build your career ready to get a job in politics.

Get involved in local and student politics

Get involved in local politics wherever you are. Involvement will give you a great start on understanding politics as well as build connections and give you confidence. Whether it is helping stuff envelopes at your local party offices or knocking on doors and talking with residents, this is all great stuff to be doing in its own right.

Once you have joined your local political party, make sure you do go to the universities political party grouping and get involved, attend events, action day and other political related events.

Workplace schemes.

Apply for your university's "year in industry" or workplace schemes. This could give you a great chance to work with an MP for a year. Many universities have programmes like this for working with an MP or working in a related role. Take advantage of this if this is an option where you study.

If your university does not include MP's you can do 1 of 2 things.

1: You could give up (that's not the answer), or

2: You could try and convince them to allow you to try and find an MP who is willing to take you on.

If you want to go down this route to finding an MP that you can work with for a year, my best suggestion would be to write (and I mean physically write, not email) to each MP from the political party that you support, asking if they would consider you as an industrial year placement.

What should you include in this letter? Letters should include your address, their address, date, subject heading and three reasons why it would be beneficial to hire you for the year and outline any information on the scheme and how to get in touch with you.

If you do not get a response within two weeks, I would suggest sending a follow-up letter with the original message and CV attached with a brief covering letter.

Make sure that you write a well-presented and correctly proofread letter.

Make sure that you study hard.

Use your time wisely to understand parliamentary processes and procedures. Many times I speak to new graduates and they have studies politics for three years, and yet have very poor appreciation of politics and its processes. Do not be that person.

Graduate Preparations.

So you graduated, but your time at University did not set the foundation for getting a job in politics. No sweat and no worries, this is what I did. I enjoyed the other parts of University life like essay writing, Fifa sessions and evening benders. It's okay. You can and will still make it happen.

My advice is to get involved locally, in politics, and find a job to tide you over that will increase your skills. In my case, for instance, I worked in Insurance as an Account Executive handling group life protection products, before interning on a local election campaign in Bournemouth, and started my journey in politics that ended in me founding my own company.

This experience, although nothing to do with politics, was useful in making me realise what I did not want to do and what I did want to do.

So how should you go about preparing? As you are now a graduate, you can now freely apply to jobs with MP's without any restriction like assignments, essays or mid-week drinking (do students still do this?). So although I do talk about "preparing" you do have the option of "going for it", which I suggest you do as you should not put a limit on your ambition.

However, if at first with this, you are not successful, do not give up. However, ensure that you are pursuing a career elsewhere to give you increased skills. And have a plan B.

When we mean "get active" in politics, we also mean attending local and national party political conferences and related events.

Why? So you build connections within your chosen political party which will help to keep your ear to the ground for opportunities before they arise and gives you credibility at interview.

I was able to do this relatively quickly, finding a role. If you work at it and do not give up, this option will also be open to you as well.

Career transition preparations.

If you have gotten a few years (or many years) into your career and have decided that you are going to make a "go" of it in politics then good for you, I commend you on your decision. British politics at all levels need people who have worked outside of the bubble that is British politics and Westminster.

Depending on the career you have had so far, making this transition will vary in its difficulty.

The first thing you should check (just in case) is can you afford political salaries? The salaries for people who work in politics have gone up recently to a better level. However, given your current commitments, it might not be enough.

To do a quick check, head on over to Google (and other search engines are available) and do a search for "MPs Staff Salaries" and then compare it with your current salary if you can afford to work at these salaries.

If you cannot afford it, then my suggestion is not to get disheartened, but to think about other avenues to pursue a career in politics.

My first suggestion would be to try local politics and become a local councillor. If this is the case, why not?

So what tips can we offer, if you are looking to make this transition?

Assess your career to date and look for useful skills and experiences that match up with the type of jobs in politics.

Start applying for jobs straight away. There is nothing like striking when the iron is hot.

Get involved locally with your local political party (you might already be doing so).

Use your CV and covering letters to highlight the key things that will set you apart from more junior and experienced candidates.

Keep at it, and do not give up.

I hope you have found this quick overview of how to prepare for

Mr Joseph Henry

politics useful.

As a recruiter, I have seen a whole host of candidate CV's from those who have wanted to get involved or get a job in politics and have not bothered to go to local party events or other such activities.

This attitude will not give you altitude; you need a positive and engaging approach to help you prepare. Although events (events, dear boy, events) mean that you might not end up with a job in politics, a can-do attitude will take you places.

So go home and prepare for government-- sorry, writing your CV.

CHAPTER 4: EXCELLENT CV WRITING.

So you are now fully prepared for the wonderful task of job-hunting and know what type of job you are going to apply for, now is the time to put together a great CV.

We are only going to cover this subject broadly; whole books and libraries have been written about how to put together a great CV or, for Americans, 'resumes'.

However, if you need guided help and support, I would suggest that you check out the reading list in the appendix.

Below, I will present a broad overview of what you need to include in a CV that will help you move towards getting a career in politics.

What is a CV?

A CV is a sales tool to get you in the door for an interview. Nothing more.

It is a sales brochure you will use to market yourself to people who can hire you.

The most important part of this entire sentence was the word 'market' and 'people'. A CV is about selling yourself as a person to other people.

I am going to repeat this to ensure that it has fully sunk in:

It is a sales brochure you will use to market yourself to people who can hire you.

A CV is to market yourself as a person to other people. Does that make sense?

I hope so. Below I am going to cover a diverse range of hints and tips.

Write for the hiring manager, not your ego.

In my day job, I see hundreds of CV's. Now, these CV's are not bad, and they are just focused on the writer, not a reader. They do not communicate to their intended audience and do not focus on important messages.

This is a golden rule of CV writing: think about the reader first.

What to include in a CV?

Many well-written CV's from excellent candidates have been let down by not including pertinent information, like telephone numbers or names.

Now, many times it is 'copy-blindness' after looking at a CV for far too long.

Every CV should include the following information:

Name - clearly stated at the top of the CV.

Personal contact details - telephone number, email address and home address

Career information - be sure to include a wide range of roles that you have, as well as the responsibilities, achievements and skills.

Education information - If you have an undergraduate or master degree, make sure to include this information. You can list all your A-Levels and GCSEs and schooling as well in this section. However, I would keep this brief.

Interests - This part is not needed unless you think it will help. However, having some personal interests and hobbies can be useful. For instance, rapport can be built up with someone based on their interests. However, avoid cliches.

Dealing with "gaps" on your CV?

Now career gaps can be a pain because, throughout our career we all can have periods when we are not at work. For some bizarre reason, two decades of work will be ignored and overlooked because of two months of unemployment, travelling or other esoteric gaps.

Now you could get down about it, or you could find a way of turning a gap into a useful selling point or at least neutralize its negative impact.

Now, if your gap is recent, you have been volunteering with your local political party, and so you have a way of filling that gap with something applicable.

Volunteering keeps you busy and is a great way to counter a gap on a CV.

You have been volunteering, haven't you?

What to avoid?

There is a phrase that an old boss used to have as a bit of a mantra "sharing is caring". Which is a great attitude to have towards those with whom you work, live and play.

However, with CV's, some things are just not worth sharing. Indeed sharing them can be detrimental to your chances when it comes to certain things, just do not share. For instance, we are all more open about mental health issues. However, including that you are clinically depressed on a CV is unlikely to get you an interview.

Would you like a CV template?

If you would like a CV template, please email joseph.henry@westminstersearch.com, and we can provide you with a template CV to help you with your job search. Please do put Template CV in the subject line.

Quickfire CV hints and tips

There is no particular order to the hints below and always remember CV's do not have rules, they have conventions. A bit like the British constitution.

Spelling and Grammar: Make sure that you check your spelling and grammar on your CV. Misspellings and bad grammar can put people off.

Avoid career gaps: Gaps in your CV attract the attention of hiring managers and human resources like sharks too blood. Make sure there are no gaps in your career that do not have a reasonable explanation.

Spell check and grammar check: I am repeating this for a reason.

Tailor your CV for each application: Create a "master" CV with all of your useful information and then tailor this for each application after carefully reading the job advert and other provided information. This does increase application time, however, it should improve your application to interview ratio.

Keep your CV up-to-date: As you go through your career, make sure to include all the different skills, achievements and projects on your master CV. With cloud-based technology and software packages like Google Docs, this should not be any hassle at all.

Use physical copies: Whenever you are checking your CV ensure that you print a version off to check it. Print it out and post it to yourself, and be aware of what it looks like when you receive the letter with your CV to give you a chance to understand what it looks like first hand. You can do the same at the end as well.

Use the right document format: Ensure that you save and send it out on emails in a format that is easy to read across multiple platforms. For ease, if you are using a Mac, I would suggest that you edit it for sending in Google Docs on your web browser so that you can save it in a pdf or doc format. Mac's are brilliant tools, however, they can sometimes, even today, have compatibility issues.

Career maths: Back up your achievements with maths as often as possible. It adds real credibility to be able to put numbers to a vague statement. For example, - I improved the process rate of the team does not sound as good as I improved the process rate of the team by 56% saving the company £1,350 per week.

Keep to two pages: Short, sweet and concise is more vital.

White space matters: Break up large areas of text - white/clear space makes your CV easy to read for your audience, and can help demonstrate the crucial parts of your career that are useful to each role.

Short personal profiles: Keep any personal profiles short, sharp and sweet. Think two punchy tweets long, rather than a blog post.

Use a personal email address: make sure that your email address is professional sounding no bigboywilson@notgmail.com or fluffymonstertickler95@sonothotmail.com.

Focus on outcomes: Highlight problems solved, money saved, money well spent, people helped or revenue generated. All of these show that you have had an impact and can take action.

Check spelling and grammar: Yes, it is that important. Recheck. Recheck. Recheck.

Think about CV Real Estate: The top quarter of the first page is the most valuable real estate on a CV, ensure that this includes your unique selling points and what makes you worth hiring.

Avoid cliches: Avoid cliches like the plague, especially double negative cliches like "great team worker who can work on their own". Please note I am aware that most of this section is one giant cliche.

Think about font: Use a standard text format like Times New Roman, Arial or Verdana. Never Comic Sans (that's a personal one that is). Choose an easy-to-read font.

Photographs: Do not add a photo on your CV, even if you are Brad

Pitt. They are not needed, although they are used on the continent, on British CV's they look wrong and allow the hiring manager to judge you on your looks (for good or bad).

Company Logos are a no-no: Do not use company logos on your CV from previous employers, it takes up valuable space, looks a bit strange and can, due to formatting and technology, make your CV look poorly formatted at best.

The latest relevant role is most important: Expand and explain your current role and reduce the size and of older jobs as time passes. The deeper you get into your career, the more critical this will become.

Black and White: Colour schemes that stand out are generally counter-productive as the old saying goes 'the tall poppy gets harvested'.

Page transition: Ensure that the transition from page to page looks good and is kept clean. Filling text right up to the bottom of the page is going to make the CV look full and cluttered and potentially information will be lost.

CV Length: Again remember to keep your CV to 2 pages in length. Simples.

Attachment name: Title your CV with a professional and easy to use name - e.g. Jane Smith's CV rather than Latest CV or CV. File names will make your attachment look professional on any emails you send and make it is easier to find for your potential employer.

Spell check your CV: Ensure that you spell check and grammar check your CV.

With CV's, there are no rules, only conventions, just like the Brit-

Mr Joseph Henry

ish constitution.

CHAPTER 5: PRODUCTIVE JOB HUNTING

Job hunting can be a tedious and lengthy process. Ultimately when you get that offer letter and contract through the post or via email, it is very fulfilling.

In this chapter, we are going to talk about a range of different methods for making the most of your time, and how to make applications.

Daily Time Management

The first thing we're going to talk about is your time management process regarding structuring your day. Depending upon your age, career position and employment status, how you structure your day around job applications and job-hunting will be different.

There are some golden rules that anyone can follow...

Set aside a specific time each day or week to job hunt. Consistency really matters when it comes to job-hunting. If you are unemployed or a graduate looking for work set aside three 1-hour sessions each day with a short twenty-minute break in between.

Do not job hunt hour, after hour in a binge fashion. This is not Netflix. Keeping it consistent, but brief will make it easier to start each day and will ensure that over the weeks and months you will make more applications than if you did a binge session every couple of days or once a week.

If you are currently in full-time work, then this may not be possible. What you have to decide is whether to have a more extended job-hunting session each Sunday or possibly one evening a week.

The key is finding time around your life that allows you to be consistent in your job-hunting and is sustainable long term. Working eight hours and then doing four hours job-hunting is not going to be helpful, if you do that every day. It must be sustainable.

Example time-management plan.

0900-1000 - Make coffee and check emails.

1000-1100 - Research and save jobs to apply for in a spreadsheet.

1100-1120 - Another coffee break.

1120-1220 - Make job applications to previously saved roles.

1220-1300 - Have a nice sandwich for lunch.

1300-1400 - Do research for the upcoming interview.

Track your Performance.

A person far smarter than me called Peter Drucker once said "What gets measured, gets managed" and when it comes to your job-hunting you need to have something to track and manage.

Having something to track will give you something to aim towards. There are a number of things to track when job-hunting. Here are three things to track:

Jobs applied for.
Interviews attended.
Job application to interview ratio.

These three Key Performance Indicators are the only things that will track your path to success and hopefully a job.

When job-hunting, you can only control the number of jobs that you apply for. Interviews and job offers that flow from these interviews are only possible through job applications. Job applications are the only part of a job hunt you have real and total control over.

Depending on your situation, you need to set a certain number of applications each week and work toward this number either each day or each week. This number, if consistently applied and you hit your target week in, week out, will pay dividends further down the line.

Batch. Batch. Batch.

When you are job-hunting, batch one type of task, at one time, and forget about the other tasks until the appropriate time. Why? Because it's more efficient and effective.

When I discovered the beauty of batching in my own personal

management, it was a real productivity boon and, more importantly, a great time-saving hack. It saves time due to the mental bandwidth that is lost when you change from one task to another task. This 'switching cost' as it is known is the time it takes for your brain to 'get up to speed' on the new job.

Work in short batches, not multitasking.

So what should you "batch" in your job hunt?

When batching, you should think about the tasks that you are doing daily or weekly. Break down the process into a range of different tasks.
When applying for a job, you have to:

1. Find a position to apply for.
2. Log the job into a spreadsheet.
3. Read the job advert and do pre-application research.
4. Create and complete the job application.
5. Log application in a spreadsheet as complete.

This has given us five steps, breaking it down like this gives us the essential components. Now we need to combine some of the elements to help our batch. It would be sensible on this occasion to batch 1 and two together and 3,4, and five together.

Although this is not the strictest of limits, it will do enough for our needs.

Use spreadsheets.

My better half says I am obsessed with spreadsheets. I deny this charge; I am not obsessed with spreadsheets even, if I wrote this book via a spreadsheet and have a spreadsheet that tracks all my spreadsheets.

Anyway, back to the spreadsheets and not my excel-lent addiction.

A spreadsheet is a secret weapon during a job search. After much time wasted, I shall now explain why.

With a spreadsheet, you have the perfect tool to ensure that you are keeping on top of your applications, you can track those that are successful and those that are not. It will also help you to batch tasks, save applications for the future and will allow you to keep a place for all your jobs to do. It is a place to store information that you are likely to forget and keep your search organised.

So what do you need to include in your spreadsheet to help you in your job search?

Personally, I favour Google Sheets (https://www.google.com/sheets/about/) as it is free and is cloud-based so you will be able to access it on the go, across a number of different devices and is easily accessible.

When you create the spreadsheet, open up two tabs in the sheet. Call one "Job applications" and the others "Tasks to do."

In the job application tab, you will store information about the jobs you have applied for and the jobs that you are going to apply for. In the 'tasks to do' section, this is the place that you will include specific tasks for the next day, or week.

Now that you have created the spreadsheet and the tabs, now you have to populate it with data. You need to record the following information on the job application sheet.

Date added - Job title - Employer - Link to job advert - Status - Notes.

In the date added section you include the date the information was added to the spreadsheet.

In the job title section, you include the information on the Job title of the role of the position.

In the employer, section put the name of the employer, e.g. Joe Blogs MP or The Public Affairs Superstore.

In the link, column add the web address for the job you are applying for so you can easily visit it again.

In the status, the section includes either Awaiting application, Applied, Rejected, Interviewed. This will help you with the tracking and measurement of your job-hunting.

In the notes, this is a place to put any other information that you need to deal with, or might find useful.

In the task tab, you will not need much, just three columns.

The first column is the task, e.g. do research for Joanna Bloggs MP interview.

The section column includes notes, e.g. review the job description.

The third column adds the header status, and include Outstanding, Finished, In-progress.

Once you have done this, you can now start populating it with all the brilliant jobs you want to apply for.

However, just one more hint before we move on. Make sure on the top line that you add filters as it will help you to see the wood for the trees and only access what is needed, when you need it.

When looking for a job in politics, there are a variety of websites that are really useful, god-tier useful even, a few others that are helpful and a range of others that can be helpful but not very useful.

We will explore the best places to find political jobs in a subsequent chapter. Now back to my spreadsheets.**taps on keyboard** *tap* *tap*

CHAPTER 6: FINDING POLITICAL JOB ADVERTS

In this section, we cover the best websites to find politically related jobs. We start with W4MP.

W4MP Jobs.

There is no doubt that W4MP is the best resource for finding a job with an MP. Why? Because all MP's are able to post to this website for free and it is supported by the parliamentary estate.

The beauty and wonder about this site is that it has a wide variety of roles on offer across politics, public affairs, public sector and the third sector. This means that it will, in some respects, be an excellent hub for your job search.

W4MP is also a vital resource for what is going on in the House of Commons, and a wide range of other useful information that you will find helpful to your career is present on the website.

The downside to W4MP is that it is a little basic on the technology side of the website, so does lack features like email updates and 'save your CV' function. However, this is just a small negative and let down compared to the usefulness of the jobs on the website.

http://www.w4mpjobs.org/

Public Affairs Networking.

Public Affairs Networking or 'PubAffairs' to those who frequent its networking events, is an excellent website if you are looking for your second job onwards. It does have a small careers section for graduates and a whole host of other useful information that you may find helpful.

Once a month, the website also hosts a networking event. If you pop along it would at least give you a chance to meet and greet people who are working in public policy and public affairs, so you can pick up industry knowledge, contacts and lingo.

http://www.publicaffairsnetworking.com/

Guardian Jobs.

Guardian Jobs is a brilliant website if you are looking across the public sector, third sector, local government or similar sets, it is for those who are interested in a diverse range of jobs.

It is a trendy website that does also have in its nooks and crannies some weird and wonderful jobs.

It is a very modern website that does include all the features that you would expect of an up-to-date website with the ability to upload CVs to a database and receive job alerts.

The website generally does not have many frontline political roles with MP's. However, if you are moving onto the second phase of your career, this is a great place to look.

With the job alerts, it does also allow you to automate part of the searching process and get a daily email, which is a brilliant time-saver.

https://jobs.theguardian.com

PR Week Jobs.

PR Week (now published monthly) is the leading Public Relations job board for those who are looking for a career in Public Relations. Public Affairs is considered a sub-sector of the public relations industry in most people's eyes.

PR Week is as with all modern websites choc-a-bloc with useful features like CV upload and job alerts to help you save time on the job searching process, which is something that we really love.

PR Week is generally an excellent, robust website for those who are looking to make the transition from working with an MP that is open to a broader range of career destinations.

https://www.prweekjobs.co.uk/

Other useful websites.

The above job boards are a great place to start when you are looking for a job in politics. This, however, does not cover all the places that you may find useful. Below we are going to outline a diverse range of websites and job boards that you should check out (in no particular order). Other websites are of course available.

Charity jobs - https://www.charityjob.co.uk/ - this is a brilliant website for those of you who are also considering a career in the third sector. There are a wide range and diverse spectrum of roles and organisations. There should be something for everyone.

Indeed - https://www.indeed.co.uk/ - this is the Tesco's of the job board. They stack the jobs high and sell them cheap. Indeed business model is to aggregate jobs advertised on company websites and job boards and then sell advertising around them.

This means there are loads — some good, some bad and lots not suitable for your particular skills set. The beauty and brilliance are that when you search for a specific job, e.g. "premiership footballer" you can save the search as a job alert, thus having jobs sent to your inbox straight away.

SimplyHired - https://www.simplyhired.co.uk - Same as above

Reed - https://www.reed.co.uk - One of the UK's most significant job boards. It has thousands of roles published on its website each and every day.

Similar to Reed are:

CV Library - https://www.cv-library.co.uk/search-jobs

Monster Jobs - https://www.monster.co.uk/
Total Jobs - https://www.totaljobs.com/

Jobsite - https://www.jobsite.co.uk/

Job Board Recap

Just type the below into google or bing, and they should appear right at the top.

W4MP - www.w4mp.org/jobs-listings-events/jobs

Public Affairs Networking - www.publicaffairsnetworking.com

PR Week Jobs - www.prweekjobs.co.uk

Guardian Jobs - www.theguardian.com/PR-Job

Charity Jobs - www.charityjob.co.uk

Third Sector Jobs - www.jobs.thirdsector.co.uk

General Job Boards.

Reed - www.Reed.co.uk

Indeed - www.Indeed.co.uk

Total Jobs - www.Totaljobs.co.uk

Monster Jobs - www.Monsterjobs.co.uk

Simply Hired - www.Simplyhired.co.uk

Main Political Party Websites.

The Labour Party - https://labour.org.uk/about/work-with-us/current-vacancies/

The Conservative and Unionist Party - https://www.conservatives.com/work-for-us

Liberal Democrat Party - https://www.libdems.org.uk/work_for_us

Green Party - https://www.greenparty.org.uk/jobs/

Plaid Cymru - https://plaid.com/careers/

Scottish National Party - www.snp.org/jobs

USA

Political Job Hunt -https://www.politicaljobhunt.com/

HIll Zoo - http://hillzoo.com/ -

US Senate - https://www.senate.gov/employment/po/positions.htm

Public Affairs Council- https://pac.org/jobs

EU

Euro Jobs - https://www.eurojobs.com/

Euractiv - http://jobs.euractiv.com

Anglosphere

Canadian Parliament - http://jobs-emplois-hoc.parl.gc.ca/en/Pages/Opportunities.aspx

Australian Parliament - https://www.aph.gov.au/About_Parliament/Employment

New Zealand Parliament - https://careers.parliament.govt.nz/home

CHAPTER 7: INTERVIEWS

We are going to give some tips and advice on the make or break part of the job-hunting process: Interviews.

Now, interviews are a strange thing. You can come out of one interview feeling like 'the business', and then the rejection email comes in. Other times you come out thinking that your interview performance was the interview definition of a 'car-crash interview' with Jeremy Paxman on Newsnight, and you get offered the job. The next you rejected after barnstorming it.

They can be strange, unpredictable events.

What are interviews?

It is strange to think that an entire job application can come down to 30-40 minutes in front of one person. However, at some point, a decision needs to be made, and the interview is where it happens. Remember, CV's and cover letters get your foot in the door, the discussion/meeting/interview gets the job (aka- you've successfully sold yourself).

Some people do not like thinking about interviews in this manner. However, those are the bare bones of it. During the job application process, you are selling yourself.

How to dress for an interview.

Interviews have their own a dress code. Even if you are going to be working in a uniform all day at the interview, you are expected to turn up in your Sunday best. It is mad. However that is the world that we live in.

Make sure that you turn up in your business smart dress. Now for men that will mean being suited and booted, for women, this can be a lot trickier and far more nuanced as what constitutes business smart changes over time and in its interpretation. We can give no definitive list of the do's and don'ts - just make sure you dress to impress.

Tips on interviews at the 'House' and MP's offices.

I have interviewed for my job in politics at the House of Commons. I also had to get a sleeper train from Northern Hampshire all the way up to Aberdeen and then do my interview and then head back down south that evening, for more interviews the next day.

It was a real adventure the months of June and July that year. I got the job in Aberdeen after going back and forth across the country interviewing everywhere from Dorset to Sheffield to London to Oxford, in all manner of local party offices.

However, I have been to the House on a number of occasions, and to be fair it is an impressive building, but it is, at the end of the day, a workplace, albeit a workplace that is falling apart, in places is damp, is a fire risk, and allows you to drink 24/7. Some say this is an analogy of the state of British Politics. In Lord Salisbury's time, people were probably saying this as well.

The House of Commons can be an intimidating place to interview. There are police, lots of police, and you might see some people off the telly, not famous people of course. Just the sort of people that induce you to shout at the telly.

The best way to get over the "intimidation" factor is either do lots of interviews or get an internship in the House so that you have become used to its comings and goings and particular character of this unique workplace.

When it comes to interviewing in MP's constituency offices, I was always shocked at just how small, pocky and average we allow those who run our country's constituency offices to be. Do not be put off. Although the office might be a little pokey, strange, on occasion, it is still the place you are going to be working in.

Quickfire hints and tips for interviewing

Hints, Tips and Ideas about how to get interviews right or get interviews 'left' depending on an MP's political persuasion (see I can make political jokes).

I was going to label this section "Sucking eggs and other things Joseph Henry lectures Grannies about.". However, my editor advised that this kind of humour is best kept for those who read the copy and do not skip through the book.

Turn up on time: For heaven's sake, people, turn up on time. I cannot count the times on my fingers when people interviewing have been late. It does not give a good impression. Think about when you are late you are saying "my time is more important than yours" to the interviewer even if it could not be helped. Turning up late might not be a deal killer. However, it does mean the interview starts on the wrong foot.

Make sure you are balanced: This does not mean being balanced vis-a-vis BBC balance during a general election, this is about balancing out your interactions when you are dealing with multiple interviewers in one session. This can be something that is easier said than done. However, the main thing to do when you are being interviewed by numerous people is to focus on ensuring that you are balancing the questions and answers across the panel.

Build rapport: Building rapport is an integral part of any interview process. Something that is not talked about enough is how much the human factor comes into the interview process on a daily basis. People talk about interviews, education, skills, etc…

However, the brutal fact of the matter is that people hire people they like. It is one of those universal factors. So building rapport is essential as it helps to make sure that people are able to get along with you.

Take, for example, two interviewed candidates. If both have equal qualifications, skills, experience and all the other factors in play, the candidate who built up the most rapport with the candidates, who had the best affinity with the hiring manager, is likely to get the job.

Generally, these decisions are made at a gut level by people who then use answers from the interview, qualifications etc. to justify this decision.

Send a thank-you note: Your parents always told you to say thank you. Now show the world you have been brought up well. You can send a thank you note in two ways, via email or via letter. Both are equally valid, and both are helpful. When you submit a thank-you note, the main messages to communicate are your thanks for the chance to interview.

Also note that you enjoyed the experience and then note that you are open to answering any further questions that are required. Ensure you put your telephone and email address at the bottom.

Ask questions: All people like to talk about themselves. From the fishwife from Aberdeen to the Shepherd on the dales of Yorkshire to the writer putting together a book about how to get a political career, who is overfond of geographical cliches.

We all like talking about ourselves and MP's are no different. So make sure you ask questions about them, about their role, about their views and especially views on any "hobby policies" that they have.

Practice, Practice, Practice: Practice makes perfect. It really does make perfect. Indeed, constant, perfect practice makes practice perfectly helpful. So get proactive. Go to interviews for jobs you have no care about taking, register with dozens of temporary recruitment agencies to get better at sitting/standing in front of a person.

The more you become comfortable in an interview situation, the better performance that you will put on when you are "up against it" during the times when you are going for a job that you really want.

Think body language: Body language, according to some studies, makes up over 70 per cent of all communication. It is undoubtedly a significant part of any connection we make with people, especially at an interview. Thinking about how your body language can look is a hard thing to figure out. So you are going to have to do one of two things.

1) You can ask friends and family to talk about your body language

or

2) You could do a mock interview with a friend and then film it and review the footage a couple of days later and review the body language pointers that are detracting from your message.

These can be a whole range of things from ticks that you never knew you had, through to things as simple as slouching when you are talking or looking bored when people are talking.

It can be an awful thing to look at, however, it might bring up and prevent things that could stop you in your tracks as you aim for that job in politics.

Handshakes do matter: Handshakes still matter, sadly, as people do draw and infer a lot from handshakes. A good handshake is part of the "making a good first impression" school of conducting an interview. Practice on keeping it firm but fair, don't crush hands but don't be weak and limp in a handshake.

Back up your responses: Wherever you are responding to question in an interview, make sure that you are backing up each and every part of the interview process. So if you are asked about what are your best qualities and you mention being a great team worker (the good stuff) make sure that you back it up in a manner that gives credibility and shows you in a good light.

Stand up when waiting: When you are waiting in a reception area, it is always best to stand whilst waiting. Why is this? It puts you on an even keel when the person who is interviewing comes out to greet you. This is a simple psychological trick that does not put you at a height disadvantage when first meeting. This may be slightly unconventional, but it will make you look like you are ready for action.

You are also interviewing them: An interview is a two-way process, you are interviewing for a job, and conversely, you are assessing them as a place to lend your career for a while. So this is a significant and essential issue that you need to think about with yourself. When you are interviewing, you are undergoing a process to see if this would be a place for you to work for the next few years, possibly longer. That is not something undertaken lightly.

Seeing any interview as a two-way collaborative process will change your whole approach to interviews.

Ask questions at the interview: This is something I bang on about time-and-time again to anyone who will listen and sometimes to people who are not listening. Which, after half an hour, are the same people. Anyway, there is no reason for me to lecture Below are a few great questions that you can ask to help:

Can you tell me more about the team that I will be working in?

What parts of the job do you enjoy?

Can you tell me about the working culture of the office?

What would you like me to achieve in this role in the first 30/60/90 days?

What opportunities are there for training and development?

What accomplishments would impress you once I start?

Can you tell me more about the day-to-day responsibilities of the job?

As you can see, these questions are focused on the role and the team; they are not focused on yourself. It is about asking questions that allow you to understand the purpose, give a good impression and additionally help you to make a decision about whether this is the role for you.

Please remember that this was a guide to sucking eggs for grannies. If everything I have said has been patronising, please do ignore me and my ways. Hopefully from this chapter you have gained some insight. In the Appendix, we have included a list of common political questions. I hope you find it useful.

As with all interview guides this can only help so far. Practice makes perfect in the end.

Popular Interview Questions

Please see below a list of popular interview questions, that we hope you find useful.

1. What do you feel is the important political issue affecting our organisation?
2. What has been your biggest success as a public affairs professional?
3. For example, how would you prepare for a face-to-face meeting with an MP?
4. Which legislation should our organisation be focusing on and why?
5. Whilst working for MP xxx, what has been your biggest challenge?
6. Why do you like working in politics?
7. Looking at our organisation what suggestions do you have to raise our profile in parliament?
8. How would you attract media coverage (if needed) for our messages to influence government/parliament?
9. How would you feel if you had to brief against your party/

former employer in our organisation's interest?
10. What do you think is the most important political issue the press are not talking about?

◆ ◆ ◆

11. Can you explain how you would influence a bill going through parliament?
12. What is your approach to public consultations?
13. What political risk does (insert your sector) face over the next 12 months?
14. Who would give you your best reference and why?
15. Who would give you your worst reference and why?
16. What have you done to generate more income for your company?
17. What have you done to save costs for your company?
18. What have you done to save time by increasing workflow for your company?
19. What have you done that has caused you to stand out amongst your peers?
20. Walk me through your progression in your current job, leading to what you currently do on a day-to-day basis.

◆ ◆ ◆

21. Describe a problem you encountered at your current job and how you solved it.
22. What are your short-term and long-term career goals?
23. The three most important duties we want you to perform are _____, _____ and _____. What experience have you had that would qualify you to perform these tasks?
24. What other background or experience have you had that would be useful to my client?
25. What personal goals did you set when you took on your last job?
26. How well did you accomplish them?

27. What were your favourite and least favourite subjects in secondary school/university? Why?
28. What were your grades in your favourite and least favourite subjects?
29. What subjects did you do best in? Poorest in?
30. Why did you decide to go to university?

❖ ❖ ❖

31. What was your degree in?
32. What type of extracurricular activities did you participate in? Why did you select those?
33. What career plans did you have at the beginning of university?
34. What career plans did you have when you graduated?
35. What did you gain by attending secondary school/university?
36. If you had the opportunity to attend secondary school all over again, what, if anything, would you do differently? Why?
37. How did secondary school/university prepare you for the "real world"?
38. Describe your studies in the area of (whatever field the job opening is in).
39. How do you feel your studies in this area have prepared you for this job opening

❖ ❖ ❖

40. When did you decide that you wanted to do a degree in _____?
41. Who were your favourite and least favourite teachers in secondary school/university? Why?
42. Describe your study habits in secondary school/university.
43. Describe any part-time jobs you had while attending secondary school/university.
44. Which of your part-time jobs did you find most/least interesting?
45. How did you spend your summers while attending secondary school/university?

46. Why did you work while attending secondary school/university?
47. What plans do you have, if any, to continue with school?
48. What did you find to be the most difficult about working and attending school at the same time?
49. What advice would you give to someone who wanted to work and attend school simultaneously?

◆ ◆ ◆

50. Please describe your activities on a typical work day.
51. What is your description of the ideal manager? Subordinate? Co-worker?
52. What kind of people do you find it difficult/easy to work with? Why?
53. What did you like most/least about your last job?
54. What is your description of the ideal work environment?
55. What motivates you? Why?
56. What makes you an effective supervisor?
57. What is the greatest accomplishment of your career to date? Why?
58. Describe a situation at your last job involving pressure. How did you handle it?
59. What do you feel an employer owes an employee?

◆ ◆ ◆

60. How do you feel about work-related travel?
61. Describe your past experience with work-related travel in terms of duration and frequency.
62. How do you feel about relocation? Are there any places where you would not be willing to relocate?
63. What were some of the duties of your last job that you found to be difficult?
64. How do you feel about the progress that you have made in your career to date?
65. What are some of the problems you encountered in your last

job?
66. How does your present job differ from the one you had before it?
67. Of all the jobs you have had, which did you find the most / least rewarding?
68. In what ways do you feel your present job has prepared you to assume additional responsibilities?
69. What has been the most frustrating situation you have encountered in your career to date?

◆ ◆ ◆

70. Why do you want to leave your present job?
71. How did you feel about the way in which your department/ division was managed at your last job?
72. If I were to ask your supervisor to describe your work, what would they say?
73. What would you do if...?
74. How would you handle...?
75. What does the prospect of this job offer you that your last job did not?
76. What are you looking for in a company?
77. How does your experience in the military relate to your chosen field?
78. What immediate and long-term career goals have you set for yourself?
79. What would you like to avoid in future jobs?

◆ ◆ ◆

80. What are your salary requirements?
81. Who or what has influenced you with regard to your career goals? In what way?
82. To what do you attribute your career success thus far?
83. What do you consider to be your greatest strength?
84. What are the areas in which you require improvement? How

would you go about making these improvements?
85. How would you describe yourself as a manager? Subordinate? Co-worker?
86. What aspects of your work gives you the greatest satisfaction?
87. How do you approach tasks that you dislike?
88. How do you manage your time?
89. What is your management style?

◆ ◆ ◆

90. What did you learn from each of your previous jobs?
91. Please give me some examples of decisions you have made on the job. What were the ramifications of these decisions?
92. How do you go about making a decision?
93. How would you describe your delegation skills?
94. How would you describe your standards of performance, both for yourself and for subordinates?
95. How would you describe your relationship with your last supervisor?
96. Please give me an example of a project that did not turn out the way you planned. What happened?
97. Why are you applying for a position with our company?
98. Why did you go to work for your last employer?
99. Which of our clients interest you the most and why?

◆ ◆ ◆

100. What is your approach to business development?
101. How do you manage a client to ensure retention?
102. Why agency over in-house?
103. Do you want to become an MP one day?
104. How do you choose which clients to prioritize each day?
105. What is the biggest challenge you have faced since working in an agency setting?
106. What do you prioritize: retaining current business or winning new business?

107. A client is unhappy with the service, how would you deal with this?
108. What is your pitching style?
109. Have you ever done marketing?

◆ ◆ ◆

110. How do you deal with a junior member of the team who are underperforming?
111. How would you advise a client against a course of action?
112. How do you build a relationship with clients?

CHAPTER 8: OTHER CAREER OPTIONS

There is only so long most people can take working in parliament and working for an MP before they decide to move on and get a new role. However, many people do an internship or two with MP's and then end up in a variety of purposes.

There is nothing wrong with this. After all, there are only 650 MP's, so there is only ever going to at most 1,800 - 3,000 roles available.

These "other" political roles can also be seen as even "post" political careers for people who have decided to move on from their job with an MP.

Jobs within Public Relations and Public Affairs Agencies.

One of the most exciting and popular routes after working for an MP is to go and work for a Public Relations and Public Affairs Agency.

This route is 'very open' as the agency talent marketplace is always looking for a fresh young candidate to replace those candidates who have either been promoted or have left to join their clients. As with all junior roles in professional services, there is a high turnover among junior staff. This does not reflect the working practices so much as the opportunities that await people once they have a couple of years of experience with an agency.

So what do PR and Public Affairs agencies do?

The below quote from the PRSA sums this up neatly.

"Anticipating, analyzing and interpreting public opinion, attitudes and issues that might impact, for good or ill, the operations and plans of the organization.

Counselling management at all levels in the organization with regard to policy decisions, courses of action and communication, taking into account their public ramifications and the organization's social or citizenship responsibilities.

Protecting the reputation of an organization.

Researching, conducting and evaluating, on a continuing basis, programs of action and communication to achieve the informed public understanding necessary to the success of an organization's aims. These may include marketing; financial; fundraising; employee, community or government relations; and other programs.

Planning and implementing the organization's efforts to influence or change public policy.
Setting objectives, planning, budgeting, recruiting and training staff, developing facilities — in short, managing the resources

needed to perform all of the above.

Overseeing the creation of content to drive customer engagement and generate leads." - http://www.prsa.org/all-about-pr/ - (31/08/19)

As you can see, there is a broad and diverse range of tasks that are related to this role. Agencies generally provide a range of services that help clients meet the above.

For public affairs agencies their main focus is on tasks similar to those above, however, focused on the small political journalistic audience both elected and journalistic as well as aiming to engage with local and central governments.

Now one of the myths of public affairs is that they all have long lunches with MP's and the "will of the people" and democracy ends up being subverted. This, however, cannot be further from the truth.

Given the sheer number of Public Affairs professionals, every MP would be the size of the marshmallow man. In most cases, public affairs professionals claim to influence but generally supply MP's with relevant information. MP's are headstrong people and know their own minds.

What types of roles are there in a PR agency?

Generally, PR agencies have three layers; Executive, Manager and Director. On most occasions, they are called Account Executive etc. with some agencies having Seniors and Juniors. However, this is more for internal hierarchy and retention.

Above Account Directors, many agencies have Associate Directors, Directors and Managing Directors. Generally, these roles will (as they rise up) they take on more business-related responsibility.

Account Directors.

AKA - Directors, Associate Director, Senior Account Director, Junior Account Directors, Lead Consultants.

Account Directors are generally the client's primary senior contact with a PR agency, with Account Managers engaging with the client on a daily basis. Their responsibility is to be the commercial, creative and managerial lead of their PR team and acting as senior strategic counsel to clients when and as needs arise.

Commericalities are an essential part of their business, ensuring accounts are profitable, and all agreed client campaigns run smoothly to task and goals.

Account Managers.

AKA - Junior Account Managers, Senior Account Manager, Consultant, Senior Consultant, Manager

Account Managers are the backbone of PR agencies. They have the vital responsibility of being in charge of a portfolio of clients and ensuring that their client's messages are promoted to their target audiences.

They will use a variety of tools, processes and activities to shape the opinion of the client's particular audiences. The Account Manager is also generally responsible for the management of Account Executives and Interns on a daily basis. Account Manager also has typically regular contact with their clients.

A critical commercial outcome that Account Managers are striving for is to retain clients and upsell new products, offerings and time.

Account Executives.

AKA - Junior Account Executives, Account administrators, Senior Account Executives

If Account Managers are the backbone of a PR agency, Account Executives are the eyes, ears, hands and legs of a PR agency. Account Executives will be responsible for all the run of the mill, but vital, daily tasks of the agency from writing press releases, organising events, and monitoring the press, to selling in stories with journalists.

Account Executives can generally be entry-level, post-University. If you are finding it hard to get a role with an MP, a career in a PR agency might be the way to go.

Where to find these roles?

PR Week Jobs, Public Affairs Networking, W4MP, are great resources for finding these roles.

Payscales.

Account Executive   £18,000 - £30,000
Account Manager £30,000 - £42,000
Account Director   £40,000 - £65,000
Associate Director   £50,00 upwards

Please note the above pay scale are for demonstrative purposes only, as a large number of variables can change.

In-House Careers

Outside of PR/Public Affairs agencies, there are a whole host of organisations that recruit people with a political background from

FTSE 100 corporates through to small charities.

To go into great detail on all these different career paths, we would need to write a whole other book. What we are going to do is highlight the job titles available for various organisations.

Third Sector.

Charities: Oxfam, Cancer Research UK, Cafod, Water Aid, Marie Stopes.

Non-Governmental Organisations: Médecins Sans Frontières, Anti-slavery International, The Wikimedia Foundation.

Think Tanks: Centre for Policy Studies, Institute for Public Policy Research, Fabian Society.

Campaigns & Special Interest groups: TaxPayers Alliance, Generation Rent, Countryside Alliance, Campaign for Real Ale.

Chambers of Commerce: British Chamber of Commerce, Durham Chamber of Commerce, Aberdeen Chamber of Commerce.

Trade Bodies: and Industrial Groups: Association of British Travel Agents, RDF industry group, Make UK.
Professional Bodies: Law Society, Royal Society for Public Health, Institute for Mechanical Engineers

Job titles: Public Affairs, External Affairs, Campaigns, Communications, Public Relations, Media Relations, Policy, Parliamentary Affairs, Government Affairs, Public Policy and Membership - Officers, Manager and Head of.

Corporate & Private Sector.

The private sector generally only employs people in related political roles in either big companies or highly regulated industries.

Example job titles: Corporate Affairs, Political Risk, Regulatory AFfairs, Public Affairs, External Affairs, Campaigns, Communications, Public Relations, Media Relations, Policy, Parliamentary Affairs, Government Affairs, Public Policy and Reputation Management - Officers, Managers and Head of/Directors.

Please note neither of these lists are exhaustive.

CHAPTER 9: FINAL THOUGHTS

Will you make it with a career in politics? We hope so.

Thank you for reading this book. Hundreds of hours of hard work over the years has gone into its creation and I hope that you have found it useful, and I truly wish you every success.

Please feel free to email me if you have any questions about this book, your career, or any other matter. Please feel free to email me at joseph.henry@politicalcareers.co.uk - please put "Political Careers - The Book" in the subject heading.

And now time for my final thoughts, of course as an homage to Jerry Springer.

Politics is a beautiful thing to be involved with. Politics, since the days of ancient Athens (and probably before), has been a game for some. But remember that politics, at the end of the day, is about serving the people. Get a job in politics and focus on serving the people daily and you will have a successful career and be able to sleep at night.

Mr Joseph Henry

♦ ♦ ♦

Thank you for reading this book.

Could you also do one final thing?

Could you spread the love and purchase a copy of this book for your old school, college or university.

Why?

Because we would like to spread the message that politics can be for normal people. Having this book in more schools, college and universities will help with this greatly!

SELECTED READING LIST

This book has been put together through two main sources. One, the hundreds of engagements I have had with those working in politics and looking for a new career. Two, from my own personal career experiences. In short, a conventional bibliography would just not suit this book. However, we have put together a reading list for your reference and further reading desires.

How Parliament Works by Besley et al, Routledge, 2018.

No. 10: The Geography of Power at Downing Street by Jack Brown, Haus Publishing, 2019

Understanding Public Policy by Paul Cairney, Red Globe Press, 2011

Lords of Parliament by Emma Crewe, Manchester University Press, 2005.

Sex, Lies and Politics: The Secret Influences That Drive our Political Choices, Phillip Cowley, Biteback Publishing, 2019.

How to Be a Parliamentary Researcher, by Robert Dale, Biteback Publishing, 2015.

British Politics for Dummies by Dummies, For Dummies, 2015.

How To Be An MP, Paul Flynn, Biteback Publishing, 2012.

British Politics by Simon Griffiths, McMillian Education, 2018

Punch & Judy Politics: An Insiders' Guide to Prime Minister's Questions, Ayesha Hazarika, Biteback Publishing, 2019.

The Public Affairs Guide to Wales by Daran Hill, Welsh Academic Press, 2019.

How to be a Minister in the 21st Century by John Hutton, Biteback Publishing, 2014.

British Politics: the basics by Bill Jones, Routledge, 2015.

How to be a Government Whip by Helen Jones, Biteback Publishing, 2016

An Introduction to the House of Commons by Robert Jones, Bello, 2015.

The Public Affairs Guide to Scotland by McGeachy and Ballard, Welsh Academic Press, 2019

The Public Affairs Guide to Westminster: The Handbook of Effective and Ethical Lobbying by Robert McGeachy, Welsh Academic Press, 2019

Essential Public Affairs for Journalists by James Morrison, OUP, 2019.

Parliament in British Politics by Philip Norton, Red Globe Press, 2013.

15 Minutes of Power: The uncertain life of British Ministers by Peter Riddell, Profile Books, 2019.

How to be a Spin Doctor by Paul Richards, Biteback Publishing, 2016.

The PR Masterclass by Alex Singleton, John Wiley & Sons, 2014.

How to be a Civil Servant by Martin Stanley, Biteback Publishing, 2016.

Public Affairs in Practice: A Practical Guide to Lobbying (PR In Practice) by Stuart Thomson, Kogan Press, 2006.

Public Affairs: a global perspective edited by Stuart Thomson, Urbane Publications, 2018.

British Government and Politics: a comparative guide by Duncan Watts, Edinburgh University Press, 2012.

Lobbying by Lionel Zetter, Harriman House Publishing, 2014.

***

Joseph Henry is the Director of Hopkins Henry a specialist in the recruitment of public policy, public affairs and communications proffessionals.

Hopkins Henry developed out of Westminster Search. However,

after the 2019 general election it felt the right time to refocus the business on the wider communications space.

Previous to setting up his own company Joseph worked for Dods PLC, Reed Recruitment, Odgers Berntdson, Nicol Stephen MSP and Malcolm Bruce MP.

Joseph was educated at Aberdeen University and Aberstwyth University graduating with a MSc in Management, Enterprise and Innovation and a BSc Econ in International Politics.

Joseph resides in Dumfries in Galloway with fiance Cathrine, Meeko the Shitzhu and Mousey the Cat. When not writing this book, Joseph loves Warhammer, Arsenal, American sports and reading way too many political and history books.

You can email joseph:

joseph.henry@politicalcareers.co.uk.

joseph.henry@westminstersearch.com

or

joseph@hopkinshenry.com

Printed in Great Britain
by Amazon